The Original Monster Truck:

BIGFOOT ®

Scott D. Johnston

Capstone Press

MINNEAPOLIS

Printed in the United States of America.

Capstone Press • 2440 Fernbrook Lane • Minneapolis, MN 55447

Editorial Director   John Coughlan
Managing Editor   John Martin
Copy Editor   Theresa Early
Editorial Assistant   Michelle Wood

Library of Congress Cataloging-in-Publication Data

Johnston, Scott D., 1954-
    The original monster truck--Bigfoot / Scott D. Johnston.
        p. cm. -- (Cruisin')
    Includes bibliographical references (p.) and index.
    ISBN 1-56065-200-4 (lib. bdg.)
    1. Monster trucks--Juvenile literature. [1. Monster
Trucks. 2. Trucks.] I. Title. II. Series.
TL230.15.J65 1994
629.223--dc20   93-45539
                                                                 CIP
                                                        ·
                                                                  AC
ISBN: 1-56065-200-4

99 98 97 96 95 94   8 7 6 5 4 3 2 1

Table of Contents

Chapter 1

Bigfoot–
Star of the Show

Its wheels are as tall as a human. It barrels through mud bogs and speeds down race tracks. Rising high, it drops down on top of junk cars, smashing them to pancakes before roaring crowds.

Each year it's the star of 600 to 700 performances around the world. It's the star of the screen, too. It crushed a car dealer's showroom in the movie *Roadhouse*. And it crushed a waterbed for a TV commercial.

Veteran driver Andy Brass pilots Bigfoot 10 to win a race at the Missouri State Fairgrounds.

People love it, and it shows. People have spent $300 million to buy toys, clothes, and souvenirs picturing this monster.

It's Bigfoot, the ultimate **car-crusher**!

Bigfoot has crushed cars stacked three high,

pairs of dummy trucks, even a limousine. How does it do it? The answer is the tires.

On even the smallest Bigfoot trucks the tires stand so tall you can barely see over them. The tires on the biggest Bigfoot of them all—Bigfoot 5—are 10 feet (3 meters) high, nearly two times as tall as most people. Each tire weighs as much as a small car.

There's more to Bigfoot than crushing cars. It's built to race. It can bulldoze through mud. It can even fly through the air and crash land on the ground—or do a wheelie on two wheels.

Bigfoot is good-looking. It has shiny chrome and glossy paint. It sports carefully drawn original art on its sides.

But Bigfoot is more than good-looking. It also has extra protection for the drivers. It keeps them safe if it rolls over or catches on fire.

But what it's best at—and what the crowds keep coming to see—is the way Bigfoot crushes cars.

Bob and Marilyn
Chandler started the
monster truck craze and
are the owners of the
Bigfoot fleet of trucks.

Chapter 2

Bigfoot's Beginnings

The story of Bigfoot began with a broken truck. Back in 1974, Bob Chandler and his wife, Marilyn, were the ones who started it. Bob was a carpenter in St. Louis, Missouri. He worked in rough, muddy places.

He used a blue Ford F-250 pickup truck with **four-wheel drive,** or 4x4. That means power from the engine goes to all four wheels. Four-wheel drive works well in mud and snow and on steep hills. Bob and his family used his 4x4 for both work and play.

The very first Bigfoot truck, shown in 1978 with Bob and Marilyn's son, Bobby, age three.

Bob drove his truck so hard, he often broke it. That's how he learned that there was no place close by to buy parts or get work done on his 4x4.

So Bob and Marilyn Chandler started a business called Midwest Four-Wheel-Drive Center. They offered those very things: parts and service for 4x4s.

Taking Off

The business took off. Bob and Marilyn tried out new parts and accessories on their truck. They kept their own truck just a little bit bigger and better than anyone else's. They often went **off-roading** in their truck. Other people saw things on it they wanted for their own 4x4s. So the truck helped promote their business.

Bigfoot started as a nickname for Bob. He wondered out loud once in his store, why did his truck break all the time? The store manager said, "It's because of your big foot on the gas pedal!"

Over the next few years, as they put bigger and bigger tires on the truck, they started calling the truck itself "Bigfoot."

Bigfoot has changed through the years. Today there are more than 12 different versions of Bob Chandler's original Bigfoot.

Cars wait to be flattened by the 23,000-pound (8,584-kilogram) Bigfoot Fastrax.

Chapter 3

Car Crushing

Soon Bigfoot was playing car shows, **truck pulls**, and other events. The blue Ford's huge size and **four-wheel steering** made it popular.

Then Bob hit on the idea that would change everything forever: car crushing. In a cornfield near St. Louis, Bob and his crew drove his big truck over two junk cars—just for fun. The big pickup, with its 48-inch (1.22-meter) tires, climbed right over the cars. It crushed them flat.

One of the crew members shot a videotape of this first-ever car crush. An event **promoter** saw the video and thought it was great. Bob didn't

Andy Brass raced Bigfoot 10 to victory in the 1992 National Championship.

believe anyone would *pay* to see what he had done just for fun. And Bigfoot had a friendly image. Bob worried that car crushing would change Bigfooot in the eyes of his fans. But finally he decided to try car crushing.

Car crushing thrilled millions! More people built more trucks like the original monster truck, Bigfoot. Today, there are more than 300 monster trucks in America.

The newest truck in the fleet, Bigfoot 11 (also known as Wildfoot), gets maximum air at the Bigfoot test track in St. Louis, Missouri.

Chapter 4

New Bigfoot Models

The smallest of the first nine Bigfoots is the Bigfoot Shuttle. It is a Ford Aerostar minivan on 48-inch (1.22-meter) tires. The biggest is the Bigfoot 5. It bounces along on 10-foot (3-meter) tires. It's the only one like it in the world.

Stage One: Bigfoot 1, 2, and 3

Bigfoot 1 is the original that Bob Chandler built gradually to promote his business.

Bigfoot 2, originally a car crusher, has been rebuilt. Now it is called *Safarifoot*. It is a monster passenger truck, with 10 seats in the bed.

In 1982 Bigfoot 2 became the first monster truck to use 66-inch (167-centimeter) tires. The tires, made by Firestone, are now standard equipment on all racing monster trucks.

People can actually ride in back as it drives over cars.

Fastrax is the wildest. It has two engines capable of 1,000 **horsepower** each. Instead of tires, it has a tank tread. It weighs 23,000 pounds (8,584 kilograms)—almost 12 tons

(10.9 metric tons)! Almost nothing stands in the way of Fastrax.

The first Bigfoot trucks were built between 1974 and 1983. During that time the design remained much the same. Bigfoot 2 and Bigfoot 3 are like Bigfoot 1 with small improvements.

Bigfoot 2 was the first to use what is now the standard monster-truck tire. This is a 66-inch (167-centimeter) **flotation tire** made by Firestone.

Almost nothing stands in the way of Bigfoot Fastrax.

These tires are now required for competition in all Monster Truck Racing Association events.

All three of these first Bigfoot trucks started with actual pickup truck frames. The trucks weigh from 14,000 to 15,000 pounds (6,342 to 6,795 kilograms). Bob Chandler calls these **Stage One** monster trucks.

Stage Two: Bigfoot 4, 6, 7

Bigfoot 4 has a different frame. It was built on a two-and-a-half-ton (2,268-kilogram) military truck. Bigfoots 6 and 7 have even more improvements. They are stronger and easier to drive. They are all called **Stage Two** trucks.

One of a Kind

Bigfoot 5 is one of a kind. It's a monster among monsters. It is the world's tallest, widest, and heaviest vehicle with a pickup truck body. It is more than 15 feet (4.5 meters) tall and 23 feet (7 meters) wide. It weighs 38,000 pounds (14,138 kilograms)—14 tons

Bigfoot 5 is the world's tallest, widest, and heaviest pickup truck.

(12.7 metric tons)! It doesn't win any races, but it sure can flatten cars!

Stage Three: On to the Races!

Bigfoot 8 is the first of a new breed—racing monster trucks. Earlier trucks used heavy truck and military frames. This one is made of steel tubes.

Bigfoot 8, the 1990 National Champion, still flies high.

Andy Brass drove Bigfoot 8 in the 1990 National Championship of the TNT Monster Truck Challenge Racing Series. He won an incredible 24 out of 40 races.

In Bigfoot 10, the engine sits behind the driver. Andy Brass drove Bigfoot 10 to win the National Championship in the 1992 Special Events/Penda Monster Truck Racing Series.

Bigfoot 11 is similar to 10. Racing under the name, Wildfoot, number 11 won the National Championship in 1993, and Andy Brass became the first three-time national champ! Bigfoot 12 was finished in 1993. It is a **tubular chassis** display truck that does not race.

All Bigfoot trucks are sponsored by Ford Motor Company. They all are owned by Bob and Marilyn Chandler. And they all thrill monster truck fans wherever they perform.

The 1993 National Champion monster truck, Bigfoot 11

Mechanic Jay Diekmann works on Safarifoot at Bigfoot headquarters in St. Louis, Missouri.

Chapter 5

How Bigfoot Works

Three elements make a truck into a monster truck: its **chassis**, its **suspension**, and its horsepower.

The Chassis

The chassis is the frame that the parts are attached to. You can think of it as a monster truck's skeleton holding together all the pieces.

Bob and the Bigfoot engineers designed a new chassis for Bigfoot 8. The Bigfoot 8 chassis uses special steel tubes. With the

body panels removed, this frame makes the vehicle look like a giant dune buggy.

The Suspension

The suspension is attached to the chassis. It smooths out a vehicle's ride as it goes over bumps, holes, and dips.

A suspension might include coil springs and shock absorbers.

Bigfoot creator Bob Chandler works on his patented suspension.

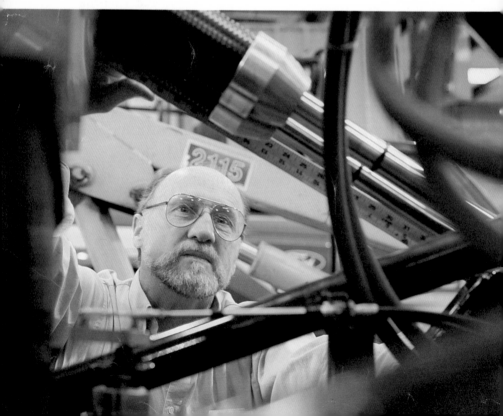

Without body panels, the tubular-chassis race truck looks something like a giant dune buggy.

The first Bigfoot racing model, a Stage Three truck, has redesigned springs and shock absorbers. They reduce the stress on the truck's frame, axles, **drive train**, and other parts. These 10,000-pound (3,732-kilogram) trucks may fly 20 feet (6 meters) off the ground. They land *hard!*

Bob spent more than 700 hours at his computer, designing the chassis and suspension for Bigfoot 10.

The Engine

All racing monster trucks must have a single automobile engine. The engine cannot be bigger than 575 cubic inches (9,422 cubic centimeters).

Bigfoot mechanics add special **superchargers** to the engines that increase horsepower.

Horsepower is the unit of measure for engine power. Early monster trucks had 500 to 1,000 horsepower. (A family car has about 125 horsepower.) Modern racing monster trucks have up to 1,600 horsepower.

Engines also have been improved with new designs.

Vehicle	Engine Size	Horsepower
Bigfoot race truck	572 cubic inches (9,373 cc)	1,300-1,600 hp
Bigfoot car crusher	460-540 cubic inches (7,538-8,849 cc)	800-1,000 hp
pickup truck	350 cubic inches (5,735 cc)	200-250 hp
small car	100-150 cubic inches (1,639-2,458 cc)	90-120 hp

Veteran driver Gene Patterson pilots Bigfoot 10 to another racing victory.

Chapter 6

Safety Features

Bigfoot flies as high as 20 feet (6 meters). It's not always a sure bet it will land solidly on all four tires. Sometimes it lands on only one. **Rollovers** are part of the life of a monster truck driver.

And yet, few drivers have been seriously hurt in a racing or car-crushing accident. Monster trucks are built with extra safety precautions to protect their drivers.

A **roll cage**, made of steel tubes, is mounted inside the cab and attached to the chassis. The tubes protect the driver if the truck rolls over.

Steel roll bars inside the truck's cab form a protective cage around three-time National Champion driver Andy Brass.

Special racing-style seats, lap belts, and shoulder harnesses protect drivers from bouncing up and down inside the truck. Drivers also wear helmets that protect their heads, jaws, and cheeks.

Special fuel tanks and battery containers keep the chances of fire low. A special

kill switch on the dashboard can be flipped if a fire starts, or if a truck gets out of control. The switch shuts off the engine, which gets very hot during an event.

The switch can also be operated by a radio transmitter so that a crew member up to 2000 feet (610 meters) away can shut off the engine.

A Bigfoot Chronology

1974   • Bob and Marilyn Chandler promote their new business, Midwest Four-Wheel-Drive Center, with their big blue Ford F250 4x4 pickup.

1978   • Bigfoot becomes the first monster truck to use rear steering.

1979   • Bigfoot makes its first paid appearance. It appears at a car show in Denver, Colorado, and in the movie, *Take This Job and Shove It*.

1981   • Bob Chandler's first car crush with Bigfoot 1 is in a Missouri cornfield.

1982   • Bigfoot 2 is built, the first to use 66-inch (167-centimeter) tires.
• Bigfoot's first car crush for an audience is a huge success.

1983   • The first Bigfoot toy, by Playskool, is sold. It becomes the all-time best-selling toy truck.
• Bigfoot 3 is built.

1984   • Bigfoot 4 is built.

1985   • Bigfoot 4 stars in the largest monster truck event in history. In two days, 120,000 people come to Anaheim Stadium in California.

1986 • Bigfoot 5 is built. With dual 10-foot (3-meter) Firestone tires, it is the world's tallest, widest, and heaviest pickup truck.

1987 • Bigfoot 6 sets a long-distance car-jumping record by clearing 13 cars.

1988 • Bigfoot 7 is built for the movie *Roadhouse.*

1989 • Bigfoot 8, the first tubular-chassis race truck, is designed, built, and tested.
• Bigfoot 2 becomes the first American monster truck to tour Australia.

1990 • Bigfoot 8 wins 24 of 40 races to capture monster truck racing's National Championship.
• Bigfoot 3 appears in Japan in the Tokyo Dome.
• Bigfoot 9 introduced.

1991 • Mattel Toys unveils its "Bigfoot Champions" toy line. It sells out almost immediately.

1992 • Bigfoot 10 wins National Championship by a record margin.
• Bigfoot 2 is reborn as Safarifoot.

1993 • Bigfoot 3 is reborn as Safarifoot 2. Bigfoot 11, known as Wildfoot, wins the Bigfoot team's third National Championship.

The Bigfoot family of trucks in 1993

Glossary

body panels–parts of the body of a vehicle: fenders, the cab, bedsides, hood, tailgate. Many monster trucks use fiberglass body panels.

car crushing–a type of event started by Bigfoot, in which a monster truck drives over junk cars, crushing them

chassis–the frame of a vehicle, on which parts such as the body, engine, transmission, suspension, axles, and wheels are mounted

drive train–the system by which the wheels get power from the engine

flotation tires–in the 66-inch (167-centimeter) size, the kind of tires used by monster trucks

four-wheel drive–a system where the engine power goes to all four wheels

four-wheel steering–a feature on many monster trucks that allows the back wheels to be steered as well as the front wheels

horsepower–a measure of the power an engine is producing

kill switch–a safety device that shuts off the motor

off-roading–driving where there are no highways or roads

promoters–the people or companies that put together, pay for, and profit from the races and points series

roll cage–a cage made of steel tubes that goes inside the cab to protect a driver in an accident

rollover–when the truck rolls onto its side or roof

shock absorber–parts of the suspension that lessen the bouncing, jarring, and shocks of a vehicle's ride

suspension–a system of springs used to smooth a vehicle's ride

Stage One–the first generation of monster trucks, which were built for car crushing

Stage Two–the second generation of monster trucks. Their frames were stronger, to survive the

wilder car-crushing performances. They had
bigger engines and were easier to maneuver.

Stage Three–the third generation of monster
trucks, with tubular chassis and super-absorbing
suspension to reduce bouncing and for better
control and safety. They are lightweight and have
powerful engines built for racing.

supercharger–a powerful fan that blows fuel and
air into the engine to increase power

suspension–the mechanical system that smooths
out a vehicle's ride as it goes over bumps, holes,
or dips. A suspension can include springs, shock
absorbers, and cantilevers.

truck pull–a motor sports event in which
vehicles pull a weighted sled down a clay track.
Bigfoot has been a featured performer at many
"pulls," and was the first monster truck to pull the
sled.

tubular chassis–the chassis made for racing
monster trucks. A tubular chassis is made of
metal (usually steel) tubes welded together.

To Learn More

Read:

Atkinson, E.J. *Monster Vehicles.* Mankato, MN: Capstone Press, 1991.

Bushey, Jerry. *Monster Trucks and Other Giant Machines on Wheels.* Minneapolis: Carolrhoda Books, 1985.

Holder, Bill and Harry Dunn. *Monster Wheels.* New York: Sterling, 1990.

Johnston, Scott D. *Monster Truck Racing.* Minneapolis: Capstone Press, 1994.

Sullivan, George. *Here Come the Monster Trucks.* New York: Cobblehill, 1989.

Write to:

Bigfoot 4x4, Inc.
6311 North Lindbergh Boulevard
St. Louis, MO 63042

46

Index

Photo Credits: